IMAGES
of England

WOMBOURNE

Mrs Boulton (centre) and Mrs Day of Wombourne Common, show Jim Boulton's 1914 750cc
Rudge-Multi Vintage motorcycle to a newspaper reporter, March 1953.

IMAGES
of England

WOMBOURNE

Compiled by
Derek Thomas and John Bowler

TEMPUS

First published 2000
Copyright © Derek Thomas and John Bowler, 2000

Tempus Publishing Limited
The Mill, Brimscombe Port,
Stroud, Gloucestershire, GL5 2QG

ISBN 0 7524 2062 3

Typesetting and origination by
Tempus Publishing Limited
Printed in Great Britain by
Midway Clark Printing, Wiltshire

Ernest Bailey, village blacksmith/farrier with a young apprentice at his premises at the rear of Walker's shop, High Street around 1966.

Contents

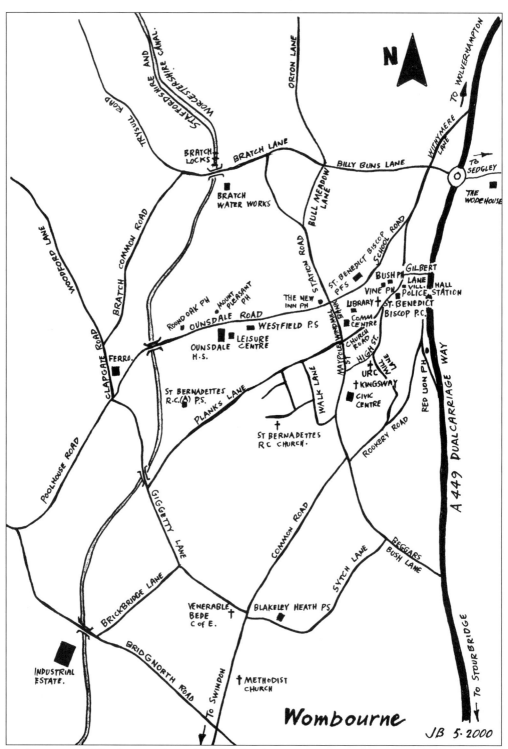

Modern map of Wombourne drawn by John Bowler.

Introduction

Wombourne is a large village, set in pleasant countryside, south of the town of Wolverhampton, and close to the main Wolverhampton to Stourbridge Road (A449). The village name is said to derive from the Wom brook, which enters the parish from the east, and winds its way through to the south-west.

The history of Wombourne village stretches back much further than the time period covered in this book. A settlement has existed in Wombourne since Prehistoric times. Flint artefacts have been found on a number of farms and a Bronze Age arrowhead and stone axe have been found in the area. The village area was also occupied by the Romans; they built military camps and constructed a road close by, which went to Bridgnorth and Wales.

William the Conqueror's commissioners visited the village during the national survey in 1086. Their brief was to discover who the landowners were, what land they held and what it was worth. As part of their task, the commissioners recorded the areas of woodland, arable land, pasture and the number of mills and fishponds. The survey showed, that at this time the village was called Wamburne, which may have derived from old English word for 'winding stream', and had a recorded population of twenty-six, including one priest. The total numbers would in fact have exceeded this figure, because women and children were excluded from the survey. The village was also recorded to have two mills, and enough land for eight plough teams.

The national survey was completed within twelve months, and was written up in Latin on parchment, using goose quill pens and brown ink made from oak apples. This register became known as the Domesday Book, and provided the final proof of rightful possession of land. Today it is the oldest exhibit in the government archive, held at the Public Record Office at Kew.

The *Victoria County History of Staffordshire* describes the County in 1086, as being poor, backward and unsettled. Most of the population lived in villages, which were grouped in administrative districts called Hundreds. Wombourne village was within the Seisdon Hundred.

Although Wombourne is still called a village today, it has grown far beyond what the name usually suggests. For many centuries after the Domesday survey, the population grew only slowly, and by 1901 it had reached just under two thousand. However, by the end of the twentieth century, this figure had soared eight-fold. The huge increase was brought about by some industrialization of the area and by the growing housing needs of the West Midlands conurbation. Consequently, extensive housing estates and new schools were built.

Nonetheless, despite the large population, Wombourne has retained a 'village feel' in many ways. The centre of the village remains largely unchanged from what it has been for many centuries. It lies round an open space, which may once have been the village green. The ancient parish church is close by. This pleasant village centre has featured several times in the press, as being typical of an English country scene. There is also a strong sense of community within the village. During our search for old photographs we have been constantly astonished by the extent to which people know one another. A visit to someone to see a collection of photographs invariably concluded with suggestions like, 'have you tried so and so? He (or she) must have some old photos of the village.' Consequently, we have not had to advertise for help in any way. A list of acknowledgements of the people who loaned photographs is given on page 128. We are most grateful for their kindness, generosity and hospitality.

Our aim in compiling this photographic book has been to portray Wombourne village life, from the time when photographs were first taken up, until the early 1980s. In a book of this size, it is not possible to cover every aspect of the many activities which thrive in village life. Using the photographs loaned, we have divided them into seven sections to try and give a representative selection. We hope that readers will derive pleasure from seeing some faces and places from the past, known or unknown, which have played a part in the social fabric of the village.

Derek Thomas and John Bowler

High Street, Wombourne. The top photograph shows Walker's shop and post office in the inter-war period. The bottom photograph shows the wall surrounding the cricket field, and the stream before it was covered by the footpath. The wall has since been removed.

High Street, Wombourne.

8

One

Education

Children have been taught at schools in Wombourne since the early seventeenth century. The earliest school was opened by the curate of the parish church in 1638. During the nineteenth century, a church school was opened to provide an elementary education for the village children. It is now called St Benedict Biscop C.E. Primary Foundation School, and moved into new buildings in 1967.

The development of the village since the end of the Second World War led to the creation of a number of new primary and secondary schools. Westfield Junior and Infant School opened in 1955, and Blakeley Heath Junior and Infant School opened in 1960 in order to serve the southern end of the village. In the 1950s, comprehensive secondary education was introduced and Ounsdale School became fully comprehensive in 1958. Primary Infant and Junior education was reorganised in the mid-1970s, and Westfield and Blakeley Heath Primary Schools became First and Middle Schools. This system changed back again to Primary Infant and Junior education in 1987.

Three schools opened in 1969, all serving a different section of the community. St Bernadette's RC Primary School opened at the top of Lindale Drive off Planks Lane. Cherry Trees Special School in Giggetty Lane also opened, and specialises in the education of children with severe learning difficulties, including autistic spectrum disorders. The age range is from three to nine years. Finally Brookside Home, a residential home for people with learning disabilities, opened. This was originally a children's home for the pupils of the neighbouring Cherry Trees School. Many of the children continued to live at Brookside after leaving school. Today all the residents are adults.

Wombourne Village School choir, winners of a trophy and a first class certificate for folk singing in 1926. The teachers seated on the front row are Mr John Apse and Miss Lewis. Olive Thomas is on the middle row, third from the left.

Wombourne Village School football 1st XI, 1920-1921. Head teacher Mr John Apse is on the back row, second from the left. The player seated at the end of the row, right hand end, is Harry Cartwright.

Wombourne Village School senior country dance team, winners of a second class certificate at the Wolverhampton Folk Dancing Society, 1926. Head teacher Mr John Apse and teacher Miss Lewis are shown with the team.

Wombourne Village School cricket team 1st XI, 1921, photographed with head teacher Mr John Apse.

Wombourne Village School mixed choir, 1924. The choir was trained by Miss Lewis, who is seated on the front row, next to head teacher Mr John Apse.

Although sadly damaged, this photograph shows Wombourne Village School country dance team, winners of a first class certificate, at the Country Music Association in the early 1920s. Elsie Thomas is seated second from the right.

Ounsdale School camp at Tyn-y-Afon, Llugwy Valley, Snowdonia, North Wales in 1959. From left to right: Colin Appleby, Bill Grundy (teacher), Charlie Bassano, Michael Jenkins, Jacko Stephens, Ernest Kirkham (teacher), Lawrence Hancox, Mrs Amy Sidaway (with Rory), Mr Sidaway (teacher). Seated on the front row:-?-, Bernard Mattox, ? Davies (with Buster the dog).

The official opening of Ounsdale Comprehensive School on 15 March 1961, by Alderman F.J. Oxford, chairman of South Staffordshire Education Committee. Also shown, from left to right: Mr D.T. Wynne, chairman of governors, Councillor J.F. Woodward, chairman of Seisdon Rural District Council and head teacher Mr H. Holroyde.

Councillor Mrs Christina Doré, a governor, presents the Dore Challenge Cup to the head teacher, Mr H. Holroyde, of Ounsdale School, at the inaugural meeting of the Parent Teachers Association. The cup was to be awarded at the end of each term for the House that did the best. Mr D.T. Wynne, chairman of school governors is on the right of Mrs Doré.

Ounsdale Secondary School, June 1957. The school opened in September 1956 as a secondary modern school. It became fully comprehensive in 1958 and was officially opened on Wednesday 15 March 1961, by Alderman F.J. Oxford, chairman of Staffordshire County Council Education Committee. Members of staff in the middle of the front row, from left to

Wombourne Village School and school master's house, School Road, in 1945 from the recreation ground, which is now part of Wombourne's churchyard. The crossing beacons shown were introduced nationwide in 1934, by the then Minister of Tranport, Leslie Hore-Belisha. The beacons subsequently became known as Belisha Beacons.

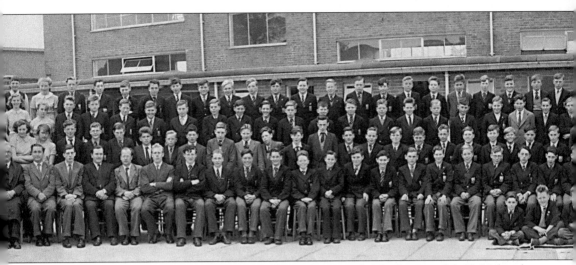

right: Miss R. Snow, Miss E. Smart, Mrs M. Sharpe (secretary), Mrs Pearson, Mr H. Holroyde (head teacher), Mr R. Foster, Mr R. Lewis, Mr N. Hendra, Mr N. Sidaway, Mr G. Morris. Middle row, extreme left: Mrs Grimshaw, Mr Grimshaw (caretaker) and Mrs Caddick (head cook).

Wombourne Village School in the course of being demolished, after the official opening of a new school building in 1974.

Wombourne Pre-School Playgroup, activities indoors and outdoors around 1964. The playgroup was set up in February 1963, and started with £10 and a few pencils. It met in the local Guide Hut.

Children and helpers of Wombourne Pre-School Playgroup meeting at the Venerable Bede church premises in December 1975. The helpers, standing left to right: Barbara Tromans, Joan Beedle (supervisor), Joan Patterson, Diane Spreadbury, Rosemary Walker.

The entire cast of the nativity play presented by Wombourne Pre-School Playgroup at the Venerable Bede, December 1975.

Children and helpers of the Wombourne Pre-School Playgroup meeting at the Civic Centre in the mid-1970s. The helpers, from left to right: Val Brown, Doris Birch, Chris Whatton (supervisor), Geraldine Hammonds, Mary Pearson, Judith Front, Dora Wooldridge.

Helpers of the Wombourne Pre-School Playgroup at the Civic Centre prepare for the Christmas party 1981. From left to right: Chris Whatton (supervisor), Judith Frost, Dora Wooldridge with Suzy, Marion Sturmey, Denise Harris, Doris Birch, Val Brown, Janice Maddox.

Children of the Wombourne Pre-School Playgroup at the Civic Centre in the early 1980s pose for a photograph after their nativity play.

Parents, helpers and children at the Civic Centre in the early 1980s for the Wombourne Pre-School Playgroup Christmas party.

Westfield County Primary School staff at the opening of the school in the Autumn Term, 1955. From left to right, back row: Pearl White, Beryl Lloyd, Mrs Wood, Mrs Lloyd. Front row: Mr J. Salmon, Yneas Dyehouse, A. Holden (head teacher), Mrs Owens, R. Davies.

School dinners at Westfield County Primary School, 1956. Each table had a server, as can be seen in the background.

Mr R. Davies, with his class of year four, juniors (aged ten to eleven years old) at Westfield County Primary School, 1956. Notice that each child sat with arms folded while the teacher was talking.

Westfield County Primary School football team, with the Association Cup, which they won in the 1959-1960 season. Back row, left end: Michael Salmon, fifth from the end is Ray Rowley. Front row, left end: Gordon Johnson and next to him is Robert Prior.

Westfield County Primary School production of *The Pied Piper of Hamelin* in the school hall, 1963. The rats were headed by Jane Hoskin and other members of the cast included: Christopher Moule as the mayor, Carol Whittingham as the Pied Piper, and Nicholas James as the lame boy.

A group of children at Westfield Infants School, enjoying the use of the apparatus in the school hall, 1964.

A game of shinty played on the playground of Westfield County Primary School, 2 June 1964. This game is similar to hockey and was introduced to Westfield by Mr Salmon, a teacher at the school.

Mrs Monica Baggett with her class at Westfield Infants School, June 1965. Mrs Baggett was later appointed as head teacher of Westfield First School.

A group of boys enjoying milk time at Westfield Infants School, 1966.

A group of kitchen staff at Westfield County Primary School, 1966.

Westfield County Primary School, the winners of the Wombourne primary schools football shield, 1970. The team proudly display their shield, with teacher Mr John Salmon.

·WESTFIELD STAFF 1973·
BACK ROW: MR.GREENSILL MR.C.MORRIS MR.J.SALMON M.FARMAN B.KIRBY K.WATKINS
FRONT ROW: M.SHAFFERY M.PODMORE (SEC.) A.HOLDEN (HEAD) M.SHARPE A.STOKES

The teaching staff at Westfield County Primary School, 1973. From left to right, back row: Mr G. Greensill, Mr G. Morris, Mr J. Salmon, Mrs M. Forman, Miss B. Kirby, Mrs K. Watkins. Front row: Mrs M. Shaffery, Mrs M. Podmore (secretary), Mr A. Holder (head teacher), Mrs M. Sharpe, Mrs A. Stokes.

A group of children at Westfield First School, 1974.

Teaching staff of Westfield First School, 1977. The head teacher, Mrs M. Baggett, is in the centre of the front row.

Mr Peter Tarnawskyi, with his class of eight to nine year olds at Westfield First School, 1979.

Westfield Middle School cross-country team, proudly show the collection of trophies won at various events, 1980. From left to right, back row: Mr J. Hoare (head teacher), D. Watkis, D. Bailey, R. Bate, A. Bradley, Mr A. Handley (teacher). Front row: P. Bedi, J. Bailey, C. Sharrat, P. Jenkins, A. Mullet.

A Middle Schools cross-country tournament in progress, on Westfield School playing field, 1980.

Blakeley Heath First School staff in the late 1970s. The head teacher, Miss Muriel Speed, is seated in the centre.

Blakeley Heath First School staff in the early 1980s. The head teacher Mr Roberts-Thomas and the deputy head, Mrs Wynn George, are seated at the front.

Mrs Kath Ogden with her class and an NNEB student in the early 1980s, at Blakeley Heath First School.

Children of Blakeley Heath Middle School, who performed a Christmas play, produced by teacher Mr P. Corfield, in the school hall during the late 1970s.

Blakeley Heath Middle School volley-ball team in the late 1970s.

Mr John Hammonds, shown with a group of children from Blakeley Heath Middle School, on a visit to Stokesay Manor, in the late 1970s. Mr Hammonds succeeded Mr Jim Tod as head teacher, in September 1983.

Blakeley Heath Middle School under 13's football team who played in the Wolverhampton Schools football league 1977-1978. From left to right, back row: Richard Beedle, Mark Smith, Mr P. Corfield (teacher), Robert Key, Timothy Kirkby, Stuart Benbow, Mr J. Bowler (teacher), Robert Windmill, Carl Hatton. Front row: Stuart Baugh, Ian Painter (who went on to play professional football for Stoke City and Coventry City), Neal Owens (captain), Andrew Hill, Neil Penzer.

Blakeley Heath Middle School netball team, 1979. From left to right, standing: Judith Hollinshead, Tina Harris, Marion Parkes, Sharon Smith. Seated: Kay Yeubrey, Jane Hyde (captain), Rebecca Kirkby.

Blakeley Heath Middle School five-a-side football team with the cup, won during the 1979-1980 season. From left to right, back row: Stuart Avrill, Kevin Prince, Marcus Pinnock, Mr M. Henzell (teacher). Front row: Andrew Steel, David Heath, Ian Hodgetts, Stephen Summers.

Blakeley Heath Middle School girls hockey team, 1980. From left to right, standing: Susan Jones, Jackie Kearney, Jane Rock, Claire Hopkins, Caroline Jones, Emma Butler. Seated: Amanda Worton, Dawn Goodall, Karen Vernon (captain), Debbie Hyde, Lisa Purchase.

Blakeley Heath Middle School football team with the league KO Cup won in the 1979-1980 season. From left to right, back row: Martin Shepherd, Paul Rees, Warren Key, Mr J. Bowler (teacher), Paul Matton, Carl Brough, Nicholas Rogers. Seated: Nicholas Taylor, Neil Gosnell, Michael Osborne (captain), Lee Newell, Paul Macey, Jared Hale.

Blakeley Heath Middle School netball team, 1980. From left to right, standing: Sophie Puttock, Jane Morgan, Joanne Lees, Marie George. Seated: Rachel Murray, Sarah Mann (captain), Julie Harrison.

Two
Church and Chapel

It is believed that St Benedict Biscop Parish church was founded in 911, and is the only example of an English church to be dedicated to the seventh century Northumbrian Bishop. The Domesday Survey of 1086 recorded the presence of a priest at Wombourne, indicating the existence of a church at that time. Over the centuries, the original church has been enlarged or rebuilt on a number of occasions.

Other churches and chapels have also been introduced in the village over time. The Anglican Blakeley Mission in Chapel Street, Wombourne Common, was built in 1890 and then replaced in 1957 by a new church in Giggetty Lane, dedicated to the Venerable Bede. The earliest Nonconformist worship in the area was at a house in Orton in 1672. However, more is known about house group meetings in the early 1800s, at the home of Mr and Mrs Stephens in High Street, and later at the home of Mr John Cooper on Windmill Bank. In 1835 the meetings were held in a barn on the corner of Rookery Lane.

In 1851 the present Wombourne United Reformed church, formerly a Congregational chapel, was opened for worship in the High Street. Methodism reached the village in the early nineteenth century and in 1894 the Methodist chapel at Wombourne Common was built. It has undergone several alterations since, the biggest being in the 1980s when the front porch was removed to make way for a vestry. The main entrance is now on the left side of the building. In 1961, the Roman Catholic church of St Bernadette in Rennison Drive was opened. In 1993, the Wombourne Pentecostal church, which had previously held meetings at Westfield Primary School, bought the former Conway Club, High Street, and re-named it the King's Way Centre where the King's Way church now holds meetings.

St Benedict Biscop Parish church, Wombourne, viewed from Church Road during the 1930s.

Wombourne Church

A view of St Benedict Biscop Parish church. The house to the left of the picture was occupied by the Chubb family until it was demolished in the 1960s, to make way for the Wombourne Cricket, Tennis and Bowling Club premises.

A view of St Benedict Biscop Parish church in the 1950s. The arbour tree replaced the ancient elm which stood on the site previously. However this tree was soon to moved onto the path opposite the church. The two cars parked by the church wall were on an area which is now a footpath.

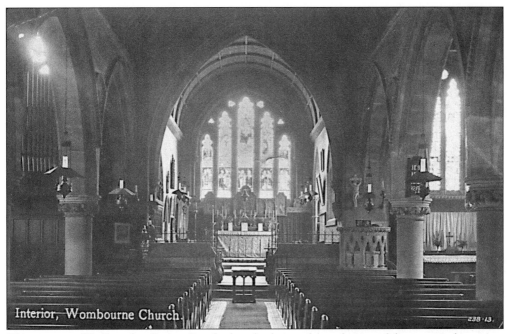

The interior of St Benedict Biscop Parish church, during the early part of the twentieth century before electric light was installed.

An interior view of St Benedict Biscop Parish church, at Easter time during the 1930s.

Wombourne war memorial was unveiled on 25 April 1920, to commemorate the Wombourne men who gave their lives for their country during the First World War, 1914-1918.

Wombourne Vicarage towards the end of the nineteenth century. The vicar, Revd William James Heale, is in the foreground.

Members of St Benedict Biscop Parish church's mothers' union, on a visit to the Houses of Parliament during the 1960s. The group was accompanied by the vicar, Revd George Meek (incumbent 1958-1969) and escorted by the local Member of Parliament, Mr Fergus Montgomery.

The Revd Stuart Huyton at the start of his ministry in 1976, as vicar of St Benedict Biscop Parish church, Wombourne, surrounded by the church choir and flanked by churchwardens: Mr Derek Martin is on his right, and Mr John Webb on his left. The church organist, Mr Reg Johnson, is standing behind Mr Martin's right shoulder.

Wombourne Methodist chapel and Sunday School room in 1965. Rebuilding changed the entrance from the front as shown, to the side of the chapel. The re-opening Thanksgiving service took place on 27 September 1980.

Wombourne Methodist chapel Sunday School anniversary, 1920.

Wombourne Methodist chapel football team, 1927.

The choir of Wombourne Methodist chapel, 1930.

Sunday School anniversary time at Wombourne Methodist chapel, 1953.

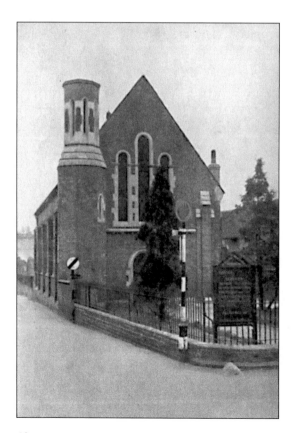

Wombourne Congregational church in March 1951. At an earlier time, the tower had a spire; it was removed during building alterations in 1914.

The interior of Wombourne Congregational church, June 1914. The organ is at the rear of the choir stalls and the pulpit is centrally placed. Gas lamps hang from the ceiling.

The interior of Wombourne Congregational church, March 1951. The organ is to the left of the choir stalls and the pulpit is to the right. A new window has been inserted where the banner, 'O Sing unto the Lord' was formerly in place.

A Sunday School anniversary at Wombourne Congregational church in the 1930s. Mr Henry Thomas, church superintendent, is standing in the pulpit.

A sale of work with a Dutch theme, at Wombourne Congregational church, in the yard between the church and schoolroom, during the early 1920s. Mr Henry Thomas, (superintendent) is on the extreme left. Middle row: Mrs Rogers is third from the left, Mr Rowlands is on the end and Mrs Dyehouse is on his left. Front row, on the far right, is Mrs Emma Bayliss.

A Sunday School anniversary day at Wombourne Congregational church during the early 1920s. The children appear outside the front of the church. Olive Thomas is on the back row, second left. Mr Hough, the organist, is on the far left.

A Sunday School anniversary day during the mid 1920s. On the extreme left are Mr Henry Thomas (superintendent) and Mr Sam Dyehouse (secretary). On the extreme right is Mr Rack (conductor).

A concert party group around 1912 at Wombourne Congregational church. Mrs Gwen Nock is standing on the extreme right. John Thomas wears the monkey costume.

Henry Thomas, superintendent of Wombourne Congregational church from 1910 to 1934. Mrs Thomas is on his right, and Mrs Evelyn Taylor, a member of the congregation, is on the left.

A Sunday School anniversary group outside the front of Wombourne Congregational church during the late 1920s.

The Opening Ceremony of Wombourne Congregational church garden party, in 1939, at Greenhill House, Wombourne, the home of Mr A.J. Allen. Mrs Allen is seated on the left and Mrs Taylor on the far right. A member of Wolverhampton Repertory Company opened the garden party and she is seated with Margaret Nock on her lap.

The Opening Ceremony of Wombourne Congregational church garden party during the early 1930s at Greenhill House, Wombourne. The gentlemen seated are Mr Hough (left) and Mr Dyehouse.

A group at Wombourne Congregational church garden party in 1950. From left to right: Dorothie Joseph, Evelyn Taylor , Ivy Porter, Connie Woodall.

Another group at Wombourne Congregational church garden party in 1950. From left to right:
Revd Raymond Porter, Miss Brenda Allen, Mrs Allen, Mr Maxwell Laing, Mrs Margaret Allen,
Mr Derrick Allen, Mr A.J. Allen.

Members of the Girls Auxiliary Missionary Youth Movement, outside Wombourne
Congregational church during the 1920s.

A group of children outside the front of Wombourne Congregational church on a Sunday School anniversary day in the early 1950s. The organist, Jim Vincent, Revd Raymond Porter and Mrs Laing, choir mistress, can be seen in the background.

A group of children outside Wombourne Congregational church on Sunday School anniversary day in 1937. They are wearing Coronation Year bows. The front row includes Bert Dyehouse, Stan Dyehouse, Mary Nock, Freddie Dyehouse.

The cake made by Marcelle Tonks to commemorate the hundredth anniversary of Wombourne Congregational church, in 1951.

A social function in the Allen Memorial Hall, Wombourne Congregational church around 1955. Margaret Nock serves tea at the hatch, Mr Sam Dyehouse holds the teapot and Doris Dyehouse is behind her husband.

The first ordained minister of Wombourne Congregational church, the Revd Raymond Porter, with his wife Ivy and daughter Mary Rose, outside the church manse – The Lindens – Station Road, in the early 1950s.

Participants in Wombourne Congregational church Sunday School anniversary in the early 1950s. The photograph was taken on the cricket ground opposite the church.

Mrs Gwen Nock and Mrs Evelyn Taylor, celebrate their fifty years as members of Wombourne Congregational church. They became church members at the same time in 1918. The party was held in the Allen Memorial Hall in 1968.

Wombourne Congregational church garden party in the 1960s in Mrs Polley's garden in Penn. From left to right: Miss Banbury, Mrs Mann, Mrs Taylor, Mrs Beardsmore.

Wombourne Congregational church garden party in the 1960s, in Mrs Polley's garden in Penn. Included in the group are Mrs Bessie Dyehouse and Mrs Muriel Fisher.

Wombourne Congregational church's Autumn Fair, during the early 1970s in the Allen Memorial Hall. From left to right: Mrs Joan Tyson (nee Lakin), singing a solo at the opening ceremony, Mrs Light, Mr Harold Cavers, Mrs Cavers, Revd S. Light. A selection of Mr Ted Powell's paintings can be seen.

The ladies of Wombourne Congregational church on a visit to Josiah Wedgwood, Barlaston, in the early 1960s.

Wombourne United Reformed church Pilot Company, at their annual camp at Hill End, Oxford, 1981. From left to right, back row: Stephen Parker, John Renshaw, David Whatton. First row: Val Davies (company leader), Kath Webb, Amanda Owens, Helen Bowler, Joanne Thatcher, Mark Longman, Louise Bowler, Susan Bowler: Second row: David Jones, Nathan Hingley, Debbie Smith, Stephen Cooper, Mark Thatcher, Pete Longman, Tom Hardwick, Andrew McQuillan. Front row: -?-, Emma Hayward, Alan Jones, Stephen Arliss, Heather McQuillan, Sue Baynham.

Wombourne United Reformed church Pilot Company at their annual camp at Basingstoke, 1978. From left to right, back row: Duncan Smith, David Cartwright, Robert Key, Susan Bowler, Sheena Whatton, Mary Parker, Andy Stephens, Amanda Owens. Middle row: Neil Owens, Paul Cartwright, Alison ? : Font row: David Whatton, Joanne Thatcher, Warren Key, Nigel Kimbley, Val Davies (company leader), Catherine Forbath, Helen Bowler, Steven Parker.

Mr H. Holroyde, church secretary of Wombourne Congregational church, presents a leaving gift to Revd Stuart Gibbons, 1979, in the Allen Memorial Hall.

The children and young people of Wombourne Congregational church present a nativity play in the Allen Memorial Hall, Christmas 1967.

LORD JESUS, come and dwell with me,
And make me all I ought to be ;
And when I'm tempted to do wrong,
Oh, give me grace to overcome.

The favourite Prayer of our late beloved Superintendent, Mr. Thomas Stevens, of Womborn Congregational Church.

Round, Junction Printing Works, West Bromwich.

A printed version of the favourite prayer of Mr Thomas Stephens, nephew of Samuel Cartwright who was the founder of the church. Mr Stephens was superintendent, from 1856 until his death in 1890.

CONGREGATIONAL CHAPEL,
WOMBOURN.

A SALE OF

Useful and Fancy Articles

WILL BE HELD IN THE SCHOOL-ROOM CONNECTED
WITH THE ABOVE PLACE OF WORSHIP, ON

EASTER MONDAY,
APRIL 2nd, 1877.

The Sale will be Opened at 3 o'clock, by

ALDERMAN W. H. JONES,
OF WOLVERHAMPTON.

ADMISSION—

Adults, 1s., from 3 to 5 o'clock.
Children, 6d., ,,   ,,   ,,
Adults, 6d., after 5.
Children, 3d., ,,   ,,

Should any articles remain not sold, the sale will be continued on Tuesday Afternoon, at 3 o'clock, and a PUBLIC TEA MEETING at Five o'clock. Admission to Room and Tea 9d. Donations or articles will be thankfully received by the undermentioned Ladies on the Committee.

PART OF COMMITTEE.

Mrs. STEPHENS	- - -	Wombourn.
,, McCONNELL	- - -	Penn Fields.
,, WALL	- - - -	Bratch.
,, PARKER	- - -	,,
,, JEAVONS	- - -	Oundle.
Miss CARTWRIGHT	- - -	Wombourn.

Proceeds to go towards a debt of £100 incurred in making the Chapel safer and more comfortable.

A programme for a sale of fancy articles in 1877 at Wombourne Congregational church.

Three
Industry and Commerce

Agriculture was the basis of the local economy for many centuries. The opening of James Brindley's Staffordshire and Worcestershire Canal in 1770, which went through the west of the parish, opened up the area to trade. Despite this, Wombourne remained largely an agricultural area, untouched by the early Industrial Revolution. However there was still an element of industry amongst the community. Iron making began in the area as early as the sixteenth century and nail making was taking place during the early seventeenth century. This form of cottage industry was widespread in the Wombourne area by the early nineteenth century, and continued to flourish until the closing years of that century, at which point the nailers could no longer compete with cheaper, machine-made nails.

The arrival of the railway in 1925 had little effect upon the rural character of the village. During the twentieth century, particularly the second half, the western part of the area became industrialised. Ferro (Great Britain) Ltd, a subsidiary of the Ferro Corporation of America, opened a factory at Ounsdale in 1935 and after the end of the Second World War, in 1945, the Smestow Bridge and Heath Mill industrial estates were opened. The latest industrial area is the Wombourne Enterprise Park.

Smallbrook Farmhouse and fields, on a wintry afternoon, 1979.

Smallbrook Farm buildings, on a wintry day in the 1960s.

Bill Boulton's Garage, Lloyd Hill around 1920. A rudder from a First World War fighter plane was used to make the garage sign.

GREAT WESTERN RAILWAY

On MONDAY, MAY 11th, 1925
A NEW LINE BETWEEN
DUNSTALL PARK
AND
BRETTELL LANE
WILL BE
OPENED

FOR PASSENGER, PARCELS AND GOODS TRAFFIC.
(Parcels and Goods Traffic will not be dealt with at the Halts).

THE PASSENGER TRAIN SERVICE WILL BE AS UNDER :—

WEEK-DAYS ONLY. RAIL MOTOR CAR (ONE CLASS ONLY).

	A.M.	A.M.	A.M.		A.M.		A.M.	P.M.	P.M.	P.M
LONDON (Paddington) dep.	12A10	—		9 10	—		11 10	2 10	—	6 10
BIRMINGHAM (Snow Hill) ..	6 5	6 30	8 25	11 15	11B25		2 23	4 15	5 15	8 15
WOLVERHAMPT'N (L.L.) arr.	6 27	7 10	8 51	11 34	11B59		2 42	4 34	5 52	8 34
SHREWSBURY .. dep.	—	—	7 40	10 52	11 25		1 43	3 30	4 33	6 28
WELLINGTON ..	—	—	8C25	10 53	11 49		1C20	3 57	4 52	7C20
WOLVERHAMPT'N (L.L.) arr.	—	—	8 28	11 30	12 16		2 23	4 40	5 20	7 14

	A.M.	A.M.	A.M.	A.M.	A.M.	A.M.		P.M.	P.M.	P.M.
WOLVERHAMPTON (L.L.) dep.	6 55	8 10	9 20	11 50	12 50	3 2		4 45	5 58	8 50
DUNSTALL PARK ..	6 58	8 13	9 23	11 53	12 53	3 5		4 48	6 1	8 53
TETTENHALL ..	7 5	8 20	9 30	12 0	1 0	3 12		4 55	6 8	9 0
COMPTON HALT ..	7 8	8 23	9 33	12 3	1 3	3 15		4 58	6 11	9 3
PENN HALT ..	7 13	8 28	9 38	12 8	1 8	3 20		5 3	6 16	9 8
WOMBOURN ..	7 17	8 33	9 44	12 14	1 14	3 26		5 9	6 22	9 14
HIMLEY ..		8 38	9 49	12 19	1 19	3 31		5 14	6 27	9 19
GORNAL HALT ..		8 44	—	12 25	1 25	3 37		5 20	6 33	9 26
PENSNETT HALT ..		8 47	—	12 28	1 28	3 40		5 23	6 36	9 30
BROMLEY HALT ..		8 50	—	12 31	1 31	3 43		5 26	6 39	9 34
BROCKMOOR HALT ..		8 53	—	12 34	1 34	3 46		5 29	6 42	9 38
BRETTELL LANE ..		8 55	10 0	12 37	1 37	3 49		5 32	6 45	9 41
STOURBRIDGE JUNCT. .. arr.		8 59	10 4	12 41	1 41	3 53		5D41	6 49	9 45
STOURBRIDGE JUNCT. dep.		9 12	10 15	12 45	2 3	4 5		5 49	7 11	10E17
KIDDERMINSTER .. arr.		9 32	10 32	1 0	2 22	4 19		6 3	7 25	10E29
WORCESTER { F'g'te St.)		—	10 56			4 55		6 57	8 14	10F53
{ Shrub Hill }		10 6		1 55	2 52					
STOURBRIDGE JUNCT. dep.		9 10	10 10	12 54	1 50	4 5		6 0	7 30	10 20
BIRMINGHAM (Snow H.) arr.		9 50	10 35	1 20	2 30	4 31		6 25	8 7	11 3
LONDON (Paddington) ..		12 5	2 0	4G20	5 5	8 5		10 15		3 30

		A.M.	A.M.	A.M.	A.M.	A.M.	P.M.	P.M.	P.M.
LONDON (Paddington) dep.	..	12A10	—	6 30	9 45	11 10	12G45	2 10	4G45
BIRMINGHAM (Snow H.) ..		6 25	8 7	10 40	1 0	1 23	3 48	5 40	7H53
STOURBRIDGE JUNCT. arr.		7 7	8 50	11 17	1 25	2 7	4 13	6 6	8H34
WORCESTER { Shrub Hill dep.		—	—	—	—	12 50	—	—	—
{ F'g'te St.		—	7 50	10 45	12 10	—	3 23	5 16	7 30
KIDDERMINSTER ..		6 50	8 50	11 11	12 38	1 45	4 15	5 44	7 59
STOURBRIDGE JUNCT. arr.		7 8	9 7	11 21	12 49	2 3	4 32	5 55	8 10

		A.M.	A.M.	A.M.	P.M.	P.M.	P.M.	P.M.	P.M.
STOURBRIDGE JUNCT. dep.		7 22	9 15	11 44	1 35	2 20	4 38	6D15	8 40
BRETTELL LANE ..		7 27	9 19	11 49	1 40	2 25	4 43	6 25	8 45
BROCKMOOR HALT ..		7 30	9 22	11 52	1 43	2 28	4 46	6 28	8 49
BROMLEY HALT ..		7 33	9 25	11 55	1 46	2 31	4 49	6 31	8 53
PENSNETT HALT ..		7 36	9 28	11 58	1 49	2 34	4 52	6 34	8 57
GORNAL HALT ..		7 39	9 31	12 1	1 52	2 37	4 55	6 37	9 1
HIMLEY ..		7 44	9 36	12 6	1 57	2 42	5 0	6 42	9 6
WOMBOURN ..	7 25	7 51	9 48	12 13	2 5	2 49	5 8	6 48	9 13
PENN HALT..	7 30	7 56	9 53	12 18	2 10	—	5 13	—	9 20
COMPTON HALT ..	7 35	8 1	9 58	12 23	2 15	—	5 18	—	9 27
TETTENHALL ..	7 38	8 4	10 1	12 26	2 18	2 58	5 21	6 58	9 30
DUNSTALL PARK ..	7 47	8 12	10 9	12 34	2 26	—	5 29	—	9 38
WOLVERHAMPTON (L.L.) arr.	7 50	8 15	10 12	12 37	2 31	3 8	5 32	7 7	9 41
WOLVERHAMPT'N (L.L.) dep.	—	8 55	—	1 38	2 47	3 15	5 45	8 40	9 55
WELLINGTON .. arr.	—	9J41	10C51	2L46	3 13	4 0	6 27	9 7	10 40
SHREWSBURY ..	—	9 33	11C15	2 13	3 31	4K26	7P15	9 22	10 55
WOLVERHAMPT'N (L.L.) dep.	8 5	8 35	10 27	1 40	2 37	3 22	5 40	7 20	11 5
BIRMINGHAM (Snow H.) arr.	8 43	8 55	10 50	2 22	3 16	3 50	6 20	7 39	11 38
LONDON (Paddington) ..		11 0	2 0	5 5				10 15	3 30

A—Monday mornings excepted. B—On Saturdays Birmingham depart 12.0 noon, Wolverhampton arrive 12.40 p.m.
C—Passengers change at Dunstall Park. D—Passengers change at Brettell Lane. E—Thursdays and Saturdays only;
other days Stourbridge Junction depart 10.20 p.m. Kidderminster arrive 10.34 p.m. F—Thursdays and Saturdays only.
G—Via Worcester. H—On Saturdays Birmingham depart 7.18 p.m., Stourbridge Junction arrive 8.0 p.m. J—Wolver-
hampton depart 9.2 a.m. K—Wolverhampton depart 3.51 p.m. L—Wolverhampton depart 2.5 p.m. on Saturdays
Wolverhampton depart 1.16 p.m., Wellington arrive 1.49 p.m. P—Wolverhampton depart 6.40 p.m.

For further information application should be made at the Stations : or with regard to Passenger and Parcels Traffic to
Mr. A. Brook, Divisional Superintendent, G.W.R., Birmingham, or to Mr. R. H. Nicholls, Superintendent of the Line,
G.W.R., Paddington, W.2; and in reference to Goods Traffic to Mr. W. J. Milford, District Goods Manager, G.W.R.,
Birmingham, or Mr. E. Ford, Chief Goods Manager, G.W.R., Paddington, W.2.

PADDINGTON STATION.
April. 1925.

FELIX J. C. POLE,
General Manager.

A Great Western Railway timetable, on the occasion of the opening of the new railway line between Dunstall Park, Wolverhampton and Brettell Lane, Stourbridge.

A delivery van for Golden Arrow Cycles, Wombourne, owned by Mr R.S. Denscombe, who had a shop for selling and repairing cycles in Maypole Street, in the 1940s. The lady shown, is Dorothy Denscombe, youngest sister of Ron Denscombe. His elder sister, Alice, is sitting in the van.

Sunbeam motorcycle testers at Walker's tea room, High Street, a favourite calling place for the Wolverhampton based testers in the mid 1920s. Second from the front is Tommy Deadman, a well-known local competition rider and tester who lived in Wombourne.

A 1950 Bedford, five-ton tipper lorry, owned by Jim Boulton's Starkey's Transport Company, Willenhall, shown on the path between Jim's home (Church View) and Wombourne Village School in the 1950s.

A 1957 Guy Warrior tipper lorry, owned by F.G. Davis of Brick Bridge, a well-known local contractor who had a large fleet of lorries.

Mr H.W. (Bill) Boulton, on one of the few Penn Nib motorcycles, built at his Penn Garage, Lloyd Hill, 1923.

The Bratch, Wombourne.

An early view of the Bratch waterworks, built in the mid-1890s by Bilston Urban District Council.

On completion of the Bratch waterworks, built by Bilston UDC, a medal was struck to commemorate this, another milestone in Bilston's history. Side one of the medal shows Bilston Technical Science and Art Schools, which opened in 1897, with the words 'Let Bilston flourish.'

Side two of the medal shows Bilston Waterworks (at the Bratch, Wombourne). Supply began on 2 July 1896 and was completed in 1897, Queen Victoria's Diamond Jubilee Year; this medal reads, 'God save the Queen.'

Under an 1893 Act, a waterworks was built beside the canal at the Bratch, by Bilston UDC, to supply Bilston, and later Wombourne. Parts were brought in by canal, and the coal used to fuel the pumps was subsequently shipped along the waterway. Pumping began in 1896 and houses in Wombourne village were connected to the mains in 1897-1878. The top photograph shows the sinking of the borehole. The bottom photograph shows Bilston councillors and water company officials on a site visit to the Bratch around 1895.

Two aerial views of Ferro (Great Britain) Ltd's factory at Ounsdale in the 1950s. The company was established in 1929 to sell vitreous enamels made in the Rotterdam factory, and operated initially from the managing director's house in Ounsdale Road. In the top photograph, Clapgate Road leading to Woodford Lane is shown in the top half of the picture. In the bottom photograph, Bratch Common Road can be seen in the top of the picture, along with the sand quarry.

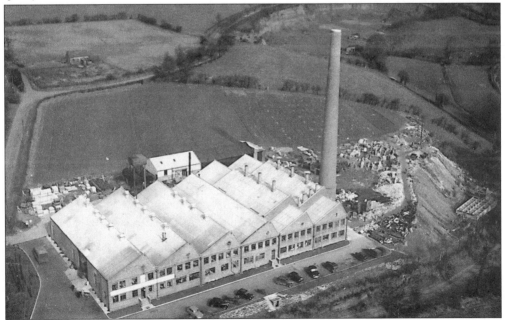

The Ferro Company's site, at the start of the Second World War. The company's first office was located in the small building in the centre. It was divided into two sections: one for Mr Marshall, sales representative, and one for office staff. In the foreground are slit trenches, dug as part of war defences.

The first smelt from the Ferro Company's first furnace, taken on 14 October 1935. Mr Marshall, with his wife on his right, is standing behind daughter Josie, who is tapping the furnace. Mr Robert B. Schaal, who came to England from company headquarters in Cleveland, Ohio, to advise on the building of the furnace, is standing in the centre (with glasses), next to his wife. Mr Harvey Trott (office) is on his left. Mr Arthur Murdoch (technical) is on the extreme left. Others people are guests and factory employees.

Female office staff at Ferro Enamels in the early 1950s.

A view of the entrance to Ferro Enamels, July 1968.

Old sand workings, Poolhouse Road, Wombourne, July 1968. The Ferro chimney stack can be seen in the distance. The area has now been developed as the Poolhouse housing estate.

Bridgnorth Road, Wombourne, July 1968, showing Redland Pipes factory.

Four

Sport and Recreation

Wombourne Cricket, Tennis and Bowling Club, has been based on land at the centre of the village since 1910. Originally the site was rented from the Shaw Hellier family, but in 1945 the family conveyed the site to the County Council to ensure that it should remain as a permanent space for sport and recreation in the village.

The club's four-acre site is often described as the village green. It is surrounded by old houses and cottages, which provide a typical setting for a village scene. In addition to sporting opportunities, social membership is available for the enjoyment of entertainment, dances, live music, excursions, quiz leagues, darts, dominoes, and food and drink.

Wombourne Hockey Club was formed in 1910 and matches were played on the Maypole Street side of the village cricket ground. The club moved to its present site at Pendeford Lane, Wolverhampton in 1965, but retained the name Wombourne Hockey Club.

Over the years football has been played in different parts of the village and in a variety of leagues, such as the Church and Chapel League and Wolverhampton Amateur League. Wombourne Olympic Football Club, formed in 1990, now plays in the Stourbridge, Bilston and Beacon Leagues.

The range of sporting activities compared to earlier days has increased considerably. At Wombourne Leisure Centre in Ounsdale Road, swimming, badminton, basketball, table tennis, football, short tennis and trampolining are offered, as well as a range of fitness activities. Squash and racketball are available at the King's Way Centre, High Street.

A village sports day on Wombourne cricket field to commemorate the Festival of Britain, 1951. Edward Bailey breasts the tape in front of Roger Davies and Bobby Fellows. Coming in fourth is Michael Fellows.

Spectators enjoying the Festival of Britain Village Sports Day on Wombourne cricket field, August 1951.

Tom Rogers with a cup, won by the village bowls team around 1930.

Peter 'Pip' Harris' Norton Watsonian racing sidecar outfit, outside his father's garage, School Road, Wombourne. Pip Harris was a well-known international racing motorcyclist from the late 1940s to the 1960s.

A side view of Pip Harris' Norton Watsonian racing outfit around 1950.

Duggie Wood of Mount Road, Wombourne, a great AJS motorcycle enthusiast, shown racing his 7R model at Cadwell Park, 1952.

Wombourne Parish Church Football Club, winners of the Knockout Cup, Church and Chapel league in the 1925-1926 season. Team members included Henry Thomas, Billy Day, George Walker, Len Collins and Arthur Hooks.

Wombourne Village cricket team, at their playing field on the Wodehouse Estate, around 1875. The Cricket Club moved to its present ground, in the centre of the village, in 1901. From left to right, standing: the butler from the Wodehouse Estate holding a bicycle; -?-, J. Beddard, T.W. Street (organist at the parish church), B. Rogers, R. Cartwright, ? Rogers, C. Fletcher, ? Wooldridge (retired grocer), W. Salter, H. Sadler, Fred Bayliss, Col. T.B. Shaw-Hellier, Bob Walker (scorer). Seated on the bench: H. Deans (landlord at the Vine), H. Carrier, -?-. Seated on the grass: H. Sadler (secretary), J. Bates.

A match in progress at Wombourne cricket field on 1 August 1910. The cottage on the left background was demolished to make way for the present car park. Netley House can be seen on the far right.

Wombourne Cricket Club around 1927. Those shown include John Apse, Arthur Hooks, John Thomas, Mr Barratt (umpire), Bill Barratt, Ernest Sadler, Harold Barratt, and Horace Sadler (secretary).

On August Bank Holiday Monday, 1949, Wolverhampton Wanderers FC, winners of the FA Cup, brought the trophy to the annual cricket match with Wombourne Cricket Club. The two teams were photographed together before the start of the game. From left to right, back row: J. Mullen, H. Day, D. Clarke, C. Kirkham, A. Mclean, ? Stevenson. Middle row: Mr Marshall (umpire), J. Bannister, A. Wilkes, S. Smythe, A. Polk, V. Harrison, J. Paxton, T. Springthorpe, J. Nelson, W. Guest (umpire). Front row: J. Hancocks, H. Trott, S. Cullis, G. Bayliss, W. Wright, J. Sparks, W. Crook, F. Corns.

Wombourne Cricket Club 2nd X1 1957. From left to right, standing: Arthur Vaughan (umpire), Roger Rudman, Chris Hudson, Colin Vincent, Tony Bailey, Tom Hetherington, Edward Bailey. Seated: Stan Lewis, ? Arthur Vaughan (captain), Fred Jordan, David Greenway.

A cricket match in progress at Wombourne, 1970.

A girls volley-ball match in progress on the grounds of Ounsdale School, 1980. For several years, an annual volley-ball tournament was held for teams from different parts of the country, and from overseas. Visiting teams camped on the school field.

Wombourne Wodehouse. The Wodehouse Estate dates from the twelfth century. In its early days, Wombourne Cricket Club played on a field on the Wodehouse Estate. They moved to their present ground, in the centre of the village, in 1901 when Col. T.B. Shaw-Hellier, the owner of the Wodehouse, rented the site to the club. In 1945, Evelyn Shaw-Hellier transferred the site to the County Council, to ensure a permanent ground for sport in the village.

Five

Leisure and Village Life

The photographs in this section cover only a small proportion of the many clubs and activities which flourish in the village. Visitors to Wombourne Library will note the large range of clubs, societies and other organizations which meet in the area.

Wombourne residents have always tended to make their own entertainment (as exemplified in Mrs Doré's over 60s concert parties, which were held originally in the Village Hall). The hall was also used for village dances. The Youth and Community Centre was opened on 16 March 1964, by Alderman F.J. Oxford, chairman of Staffordshire County Council Education Committee. The centre is run by the council and is available to all sections of the community. The Wombourne Players meet there and regularly perform plays in the hall. The centre is also the venue for the Village Youth Club. There are also facilities for concerts, dances and meetings, provided by the Civic Centre, which opened in 1977.

Evening classes have been available for many years and there is a wide range of courses for those interested in, for example, arts, crafts, history, languages and computers.
Facilities for the elderly have expanded in recent years. There has also been growth in the number of residential and warden controlled homes available.

The village pubs have also changed with the times, and now offer a range of meals alongside more traditional facilities. The opening of two restaurants serving Asian-style meals and take away facilities, reflects current changes in eating habits and entertainment.

A wedding group, taken at the rear of the Sycamores, Maypole Street around 1925. The bride was Doris Dickens, adopted daughter of Mr and Mrs Henry Thomas, who are seated on the extreme right. Other guests include Mr C. Thomas, Mr J.B. Shaw, Mr and Mrs Humphries and their daughter Marie. The Sycamores is no longer a private house and is occupied by Perrigo, Opticians and Tracy Hair Design on one side, and by the Staffordshire Building Society and David Stephenson, Solicitors, on the other side.

A Wombourne wedding around 1925. The bride is Nellie Law. The lady on the far left is Mrs Hale and the lady on the far right is Mary Law.

Mr Frank Parnwell, head gardener at the Wodehouse, shown in a greenhouse with a magnificent display of chrysanthemums, 1912.

A gathering on the recreation ground with a 'widow and orphans' banner on display during the 1930s.

George Waite (on the right) with a Sunbeam cycle, and a friend with his Rudge cycle, in the grounds of the Old Bush public house, High Street. This pub was a favourite meeting place for cyclists around 1908.

Members of the Darby and Joan Club in front of the Women's Institute Village Hall, High Street in the mid-1950s.

An outing to Highgate Common for Wombourne children, organised by Wombourne Labour Party during the late 1940s. Those standing in front of the lorry include Archie Clark, Mrs Wood, Doris Linney, Joe Larne, Gilbert Thomas, Bill Edwards and Henry Thomas.

Mrs Christina Doré of Walk Lane, Wombourne, reading a letter received from the Queen in 1953. Mrs Doré had written and sent to the Queen a poem called, 'Daughter of Britain' composed for the Coronation Year. This was one of a number of poems written by Mrs Doré, to express her love of Queen and Country.

Wombourne Darby and Joan Club concert party, in full voice for their conductor and president, Mrs C. Doré. Seated at the piano is Mrs Powell. The club was founded by Mrs Doré in 1948 and met in the Women's Institute village hall.

Wombourne Darby and Joan Club concert party in fancy dress before a performance produced by Mrs C. Doré during the 1960s.

A Darby and Joan Club annual dinner during the 1950s, with the committee standing at the back. From left to right, standing: Lucy Key, -?-, Mrs Court, Marj Day, Mrs Cooper, Mrs Mann, -?-, Mrs C. Doré.

People enjoying themselves at a Coronation tea party in 1953. Included in the group are Mrs Mann, Bob Ball, Audrey Ball, Mrs Wilson, Joe Carter, Mrs Woodhall, Ruth Jones, and Mrs Carter.

First meeting of the Wolverhampton branch of the Vintage Motorcycle Club at the Red Lion public house, Wombourne, 26 August 1951. The motorcyclists are gathered on what was at that time the main road, which has since been bypassed. From left to right: Jack Crook, Jim Boulton, Jock Bushell, J. Edkins, H. Carter, Len Wills, Jack Salmon.

The Wolverhampton Branch of the Vintage Motorcycle Club's Banbury run, 1951, for pre-1931 motorcycles.. From left to right: Jack Crook, -?-, and Ron Denscombe (owner of Wombourne Cycle Shop, Maypole Street). The motorcycle number sixty is Jim Boulton's 1920 225cc Royal Enfield.

Motorcycle number sixty, was transported to Banbury on the roof of Ron Denscombe's pre-war Vauxhall car, 1951.

Jack Crook and Ron Denscombe, seated on a vintage motorcycle combination, outside Jim Boulton's bungalow in School Road, during the early 1960s. John Perry is in the sidecar.

John Perry, Ron Denscombe and Jack Crook with a vintage motorcycle, on the recreation ground outside the village school. The machine is a 1923 2¾hp Douglas. The recreation ground is now part of Wombourne's churchyard.

A 1923 2¾hp Douglas vintage motorcycle outside Ron Denscombe's Cycle Shop in Maypole Street, during the 1940s. The shop is now the Libra Dress Agency.

John Harris, (brother of Pip Harris) of H.F. Harris Garage, School Road, refuels his Ariel motorcycle at a Black Hills Scramble, 1949.

Jim Boulton outside his home at Bridge House, Ounsdale Road, Wombourne, with part of his collection of vintage motorcycles, 1952. The machines, from left to right: 1923 500cc Rudge-Multi; 1923 285cc Ner-Car; 1914 750cc Rudge-Multi; 1923 135cc tricycle.

A young Jim Boulton, in 1925, in front of a 1912 BSA car. Before official vehicles were available, this car was used by Mr May, Relieving Officer of Seisdon Union Workhouse, to transport people to hospital – and also the occasional corpse.

Jim Boulton's 1933 Rover Special outside his bungalow 'Glendale' in School Road, 1948.

The president and fellow founder members of Wombourne Caledonian Society celebrating their twenty-fifth birthday party in 1979. From left to right: Mrs Jenny Smith, Mr Tom Smith, Mrs Anne Horton, Mr Len Hayward, the president Mrs Barbara Longfellow, Mrs Jean Hayward, Mrs Lena Rogers, Mr Bill Rogers.

The haggis is piped in at a meeting of the Wombourne Caledonian Society around 1980. Mr Jimmy Gunn carries the haggis, and is followed by Mr Keith Wilson with the toasting drinks.

Model engines at the rear of the Mount public house, Ounsdale Road, during the late 1950s. The train and track were set up by a local railway society.

Wombourne Canal Festival on the Staffordshire and Worcestershire Canal in 1971.

Mrs Eileen Powell, chairman of Wombourne Townswomen's Guild, plants an Old English oak sapling in February 1973, outside the Council Offices for the Plant a Tree for '73 campaign. Members of the Guild and representatives of West Staffordshire Federation of Townswomen's Guilds are gathered round.

Holyrood Patrol venture cooking at Wombourne Girl Guides Camp at Beaudesert, 1977. From left to right: Eve McDonald, Margaret Raybould, Gillian Wyatt, Janet Kelly, Karen Wardley.

Windsor Patrol eating their home made recipe of 'choc mallow' at Wombourne Girl Guides Camp at Beaudesert, 1977. From left to right: Katherine Raybould, Claire Bathson, Ruth Moorhouse, Sarah Forder, Catherine Huyton.

Sandringham Patrol venture cooking at Wombourne Girl Guides Camp at Beaudesert 1977. From left to right: Mavis Smart, Jayne Sharples, Suzanne Cargill, Rosalind Bradley, Sara Griffiths, Elaine Burrows.

Wombourne Girl Guides Company, seated on a log at Beaudesert, 26 July 1977.

Wombourne Girl Guides Company on the steps of the campfire circle at Beaudesert, 26 July 1977.

Hoisting the Colours at Wombourne Girl Guides Camp at Beaudesert, 29 July 1977. From left to right: Alison Kelly, Sarah Ward, Melanie Amos, Sheila Standish, Eileen Moorhouse, Mavis Smart, Helen Jones, Joanne Colebourne.

Wombourne First Scouts and Cubs Company, with their trophies won at a pedal car rally in Stourbridge, May 1979.

Wombourne 'E' Townswomen's Guild Choir with a trophy won in 1979. The choir took part in competitions at Catshill, Dudley and Brownhills. From left to right, standing: Spencer Willetts (conductor), Maisie Frome, Gwen Davidson, Gladys Bourne, Joan Piper, Joan Waghorn, Sylvia Blewitt, Doreen Pike, Hazel Perry, Val Edwards, Pat Hickman, Dorothy Griffiths. Seated: Ina Dennis, June Crowther, Jackie Poole, Vera Jeavons, Irene Blackhouse, Dorothy Whitehouse, Jessie Willetts, Vi Fraser, Lena Rogers, Edna Tildesley, Dorothy Trice. Other members (not shown): Paul Hinton (pianist) and Connie Sudlow.

Wombourne 'E' Townswomen's Guild Choir members 1979. From left to right, back row: Joan Waghorn, Sylvia Blewitt, Doreen Pike, Hazel Perry. Front row: Dorothy Whitehouse, Jessie Willetts, Vi Fraser, Lena Rogers.

A Wombourne Darby and Joan Christmas Party at the Women's Institute Village Hall around 1950.

Six
Local Goverment, Law and Order

When the Domesday commissioners visited Wombourne in 1086, the village was part of an old English administrative district called the Seisdon Hundred. The Hundreds formed regions within Counties. The title of the Hundred stems from the village of Seisdon which was an important manor during the time of Hundred government.

When the Hundreds were abolished, Wombourne became part of Seisdon Rural District and the council had an office in Walk Lane. Wombourne remained in Seisdon RD until 1974 when it became part of South Staffordshire District. It is now the largest village within the South Staffordshire District Council area and has a Civic Centre at Gravel Hill.

The Magistrates Court is in a separate building adjacent to the Civic Centre, and in 1971 the police station in High Street was opened, replacing the station in School Road.

The Clock Tower at the Civic Centre commemorates the centenary of Wombourne Parish Council in 1994.

As part of her work for the WRVS, Councillor Mrs Christina Doré distributes national dried milk, cod liver oil and orange juice, from a cottage on Gravel Hill, around 1958.

As part of a Wombourne civil defence exercise, around 1957, two field kitchens were built to provide emergency meals. Mrs Christina Doré can be seen working at the table in the centre.

WUN.22.

SEISDON COUNCIL OFFICES. WOMBOURNE.

Seisdon Council Office, Wombourne, in 1968, now the site of Wombourne Civic Centre.

Councillor Mrs Christina Doré with council members of Seisdon Rural District Council, during the 1950s and 1960s. In the top picture, Mrs Doré is in the middle row, sixth from the left. In the bottom picture, Mrs Doré is in the middle row, standing behind the chairman.

A stolen car which had been pushed into a sandpit in Poolhouse Lane, November 1956. The policemen, from left to right: PC Jack Gash, PC Les Reynolds, Sergeant Harry Phillips.

A road accident on the old A449 near the Red Lion public house, 1954. From left to right: PC John Mellor, PC Jack Gash, PC Jack Tarporley.

Councillor Andrew Ogden, cutting the first sod for the adventure playground which he designed. He is watched by an interested group of children including Councillor Ogden's son Chris, and daughter Ruth.

A group of children watch Councillor Ogden at the controls of a digger, prior to the construction of the adventure playground.

Councillor Andrew Ogden performing the opening ceremony of the adventure playground, off Common Road, near the Wom Brook in 1974. Those present at the ceremony, included Ted Waterfield, Mrs Waterfield, Arthur Suckling, Pauline Kelly, Kath Ogden, Clara Gould, Minnie Hill, Joyce Suckling, Vera Beardsmore, Jim Beardsmore, Jimmy Hill, Margaret Lawson, and Revd John Porter.

Children enjoying the ladder-bridge over the new adventure playground. Sarah Williams leads the children over the bridge.

PC Jack Dash, Sergeant John Stevenson and PC Ron Gladstone lead the opening parade of the Wombourne British Legion, along High Street in the early 1950s.

Wombourne Darby and Joan Club annual dinner during the 1950s. Mrs Jean Gash is serving the tea; behind her is Gwen Fisher.

Popular Wombourne policeman, Jack Gash's 1932 Triumph Super Seven, in School Road during the late 1940s. In 1947 Jack Gash was the only police constable in the village. He lived in a house at the junction of Planks Lane and Windmill Bank. At the rear of the house, was the only police cell in the area. Mrs Jean Gash is seated at the wheel with Simon Peers.

Local Police Constable Priest with his wife, who was the local district nurse (shown on the extreme left). Their adopted daughter, Penny is in the centre, along with Mrs Peggy Denscombe (third from left) and her daughter Barbara (extreme right). The group is outside the police house on the corner of Planks Lane and Windmill Bank, in 1950.

Seven
Village Views

Visitors who approach the village from the north, along the A449, cannot fail to admire the beautiful countryside between the suburbs of Wolverhampton and Wombourne. This stretch of green belt has helped to retain the Wombourne village character. When turning from the A449 into Gilbert Lane, visitors are presented with a quintessential English view: the elegant spire of St Benedict Biscop church, rising above the surrounding buildings of the Vine and Bush public houses, Waterfield House, the police station and the village hall. From the south, Wombourne nestles below the Orton Hills, with the Ferro chimney a prominent landmark.

The buildings surrounding the village centre have changed very little except that some residential dwellings have changed to commercial use. Housing has developed rapidly during the past fifty years. Inevitably this has brought changes to the local environment. Industries have also developed. This section of the book attempts to show the appearance of some areas of the village before the builders moved in. It also includes scenes captured on film years ago, but which remain little altered today.

The Vine Inn, High Street, in the early 1930s. The Vine had been a public house since the second half of the nineteenth century.

The Women's Institute Village Hall, on the High Street, opposite the Vine, during the early 1930s.

An area east of Wombourne, showing the old A449 road to Stourbridge with the Red Lion in the centre, during the early years of the twentieth century. The area is known as Battlefield.

Wombourne from the west, showing St Benedict Biscop Parish church and the Wombourne Institute. The latter dates back to the early nineteenth century, when it was a day school. It became the Wombourne Institute when a new school was built in 1863. Since then, the premises have been used as a village institute, a men's institute, a clinic, and a home to Wombourne Volunteer Bureau, also known as the Hand-in-Hand. The motto over the porch, 'Let's go hand in hand together not one before another', was placed there by the founders of the Institute and continues to be the aim of those who use it now.

A view from the rear of Jim Boulton's home 'Church View', before houses were built along Orton Lane. The latter can be seen in the centre with Pickerells Hill on the right.

Ounsdale Road during the 1930s.

Walk Lane during the 1930s.

Rookery Lane during the 1930s.

238-3　　　　　　　　　　　　SCHOOL LANE, WOMBOURNE.

An early twentieth century view of School Road with the village school on the left.

Cottages in Billy Burns Lane at the foot of Pickerells Hill in the early 1960s.

A view from Bull Meadow lane looking towards Pickerells Hill on a winters days during the late 1960s.

A Wolverhampton Corporation bus outside St Benedict Biscop Parish church during the Second World War. The headlamps are masked to meet with wartime blackout restrictions.

Orton Lane looking towards Wombourne, before the demolition of the cottages on the right in Flash Lane. The old disused sand quarry can be seen in the background.

Houses next to the railway bridge, Common Road, during the 1920s. Doris Linney stands at the gate.

The junction of Church Road and Maypole Street during the mid-1940s before the cricket field wall was demolished. The old cricket and tennis pavilions can be seen in the background.

The Bratch around 1960. The Staffordshire and Worcestershire Canal was built during the late eighteenth century by James Brindley. Three locks were required at the Bratch because of a sharp fall in the level of the land. The tall octagonal toll-house is in the background.

Houses at Smallbrook in the 1960s. The area is at the east-end of the High Street and the name refers to the stream which once ran down the High street.

Cottages at Smallbrook around 1970. The photograph at the top shows a view at the end of the High Street with Smallbrook Lane on the left and Gilbert Lane ahead. The bottom photograph is a view from Gilbert Lane. The cottages stand on the present site of Waterfield House, opened on 5 April 1986 and named after Councillor Ted Waterfield.

Windmill Bank, Wombourne. The top photograph shows the construction of the footpath. The low wall and waste ground on the right, is now occupied by shops and a small parking area. The bottom picture shows Windmill Bank at a later date.

Windmill Bank, Wombourn.

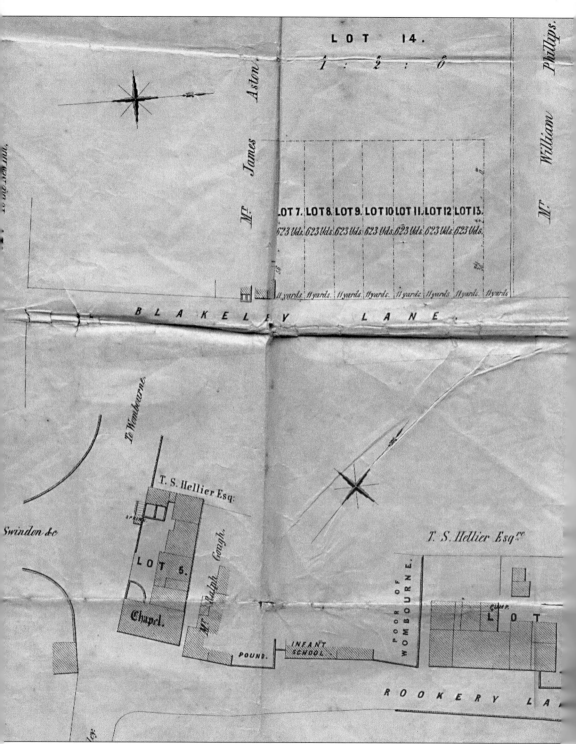

Part of an auctioneer's plan of properties and land, sold at five o'clock in the evening on Monday 15 September 1856, 'by Mr Bateman at the house of Mr Morgan, The Old Bush Inn, Womborne.' The chapel marked on the map, was a barn used by Congregationalists before they

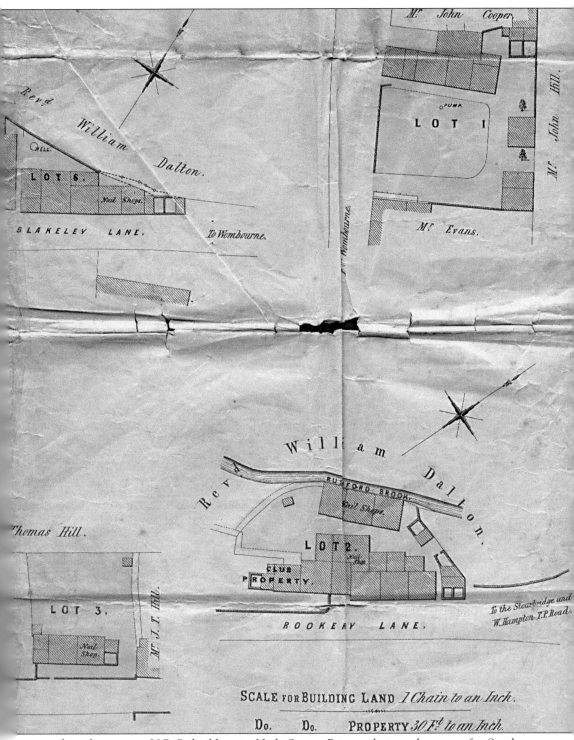

Mr John Cooper

Revd

William Dalton.

LOT 6.

Chell.

Nail Shops.

BLAKELEY LANE.

To Wombourne.

To Wombourne.

LOT I

PUMP

Mr John Hill.

Mr Evans.

William Dalton.

Revd

RUMFORD BROOK

Nail Shops.

LOT 2.

Nail Shop

CLUB PROPERTY.

Thomas Hill.

LOT 3.

Nail Shop

Mr J. T. Hill.

ROOKERY LANE.

To the Stourbridge and W.Hampton. T.P.Road.

SCALE for BUILDING LAND *1 Chain to an Inch.*

Do.   Do.   PROPERTY *30 Ft. to an Inch.*

moved to the present U.R.C. building in High Street. Prior to being taken over for Sunday worship, the barn was a boys' day school.

Cottages near the farmhouse in Mill Lane during the late 1940s.

The road junction at Gilbert Lane and the A449 Wolverhampton to Stourbridge road before the construction of the A449 dual carriageway, during the early 1960s.

Mill Lane Farmhouse around 1965. The top photograph shows a rear view of the farmhouse from the kitchen garden. The photograph below shows the front view of the farmhouse from Mill Lane.

The High Street around 1950.

Winter sports on Light Hill, Wombourne, 1963. Billy Bunns Island is in the foreground.

A view from Gravel Hill in 1964, looking towards the junction between Rookery Road, Green Hill and Common Road. The field in the background has been developed for housing. The house seen just over the bridge stands where the barn/chapel appears on the map, pp 118 and 119

Cottages at Wombourne Common during the 1940s, near where the Bridgnorth Road crosses the road from Wombourne to Swindon.

An aerial view of St Benedict Biscop Parish church and churchyard, Wombourne Cricket, Tennis and Bowling Club, and buildings at the beginning of the High Street.

The Staffordshire and Worcestershire Canal in 1964. The Ferro Enamel Company's chimney can be seen in the distance.

WOMBOURNE

NEAR WOLVERHAMPTON

FLORAL FETE
AND
GYMKHANA

President MISS E. M. SHAW-HELLIER

AT

GILBERT LANE

WOMBOURNE

(BY kind Permission of Mr G. Lander)

SATURDAY 24TH JULY 1965

Gates Open 11 a.m.

ADMISSION 3/6
(After 6 p.m. 2/-)

First Event 12 noon

CHILDREN 1/6
(After 6 p.m. 6d.)

Advance Ticket 2/- available at Beatties Enquiry Bureau and Committee Members

OPEN ADULT AND CHILDREN'S JUMPING

INCLUDING FOXHUNTER CLASS   5 CUPS and OVER £100 in PRIZES

GYMKHANA EVENTS

Affiliated to B.S.J.A

FLOWER, FRUIT, AND VEGETABLE SHOW

10 CUPS, DIPLOMAS AND £130 IN PRIZES

S. S. COUNTY BRITISH LEGION YOUTH
PIPE AND DRUM BAND
SHEEP SHEARING DEMONSTRATION
BOY SCOUTS DISPLAY
FORESTRY COMMISSION DISPLAY
SCOTTISH HALFHOUR
PONY GROOMING INSTRUCTION
Punch & Judy Shows – Bowling for Live Pig
Children's Corner – Sketch Artist – Side Shows

Adequate Refreshments available on Ground

For Further information apply Gen. Sec: Mr R. G. MacPherson, "Beggars Roost" 25 Planks Lane., Wombourne.   Telephone Wombourne 2835
Frequent Service of Midland Red and Wolverhampton Corporation Buses Pass the Show Ground

Paulton Bros. Limited, Wolverhampton.

Wombourne floral fete and gymkhana was an annual event for many years. The gymkhana was a big attraction and included the Foxhunter Daily Express National Jumping Competition.

VALUABLE

FREEHOLD LANDS,

PUBLIC HOUSE,

AND

MESSUAGES

IN THE

Parish of Wombourn, near Wolverhampton.

TO BE SOLD BY AUCTION,

BY MESSRS.

ASTON AND SOLLOM,

(BY DIRECTION OF THE TRUSTEES FOR SALE,)

ON WEDNESDAY, APRIL 1, 1863,

AT THE

Seven Stars Inn, St. John's Street, Wolverhampton,

AT FIVE O'CLOCK IN THE AFTERNOON,

SUBJECT TO CONDITIONS TO BE READ PRIOR TO THE SALE, THE WITHIN-MENTIONED VALUABLE

PROPERTIES.

Auction sale at the Seven Stars Inn, St John Street, Wolverhampton, of properties in Wombourne, 1 April, 1863.

PARTICULARS.

LOT 1.

All that Freehold Piece of Arable Land, known as the "Holly Tree Piece," having a considerable frontage to the turnpike road leading from Wolverhampton to Stourbridge, also a frontage to the road leading from Beggar's Bush to Wombourn, containing 1a. 0r. 34p. or thereabouts, and bounded by lands belonging to the Earl of Dudley and the Rev. W. Dalton.

LOT 2.

A Freehold Close of Arable Land, known as the "Ironsides Piece," situate opposite lot 1, and on the other side of the said turnpike road, to which road it has a considerable frontage, and is bounded by lands of the Rev. W. Dalton, and contains 3 roods 19p. or thereabouts.

LOT 3.

A Freehold Close of Arable Land (formerly in two Closes), called the "Upper and Lower Parkside Pieces," situate near to lot 2, on the same side of the said turnpike road, to which it has a frontage, containing 3a. 2r. 27p. or thereabouts, and bounded by lands of the Earl of Dudley and Rev. W. Dalton.

The above three lots are situate in the immediate vicinity of Himley Park and the residences of W. Chinner, Esq. G. Addenbrooke, Esq. John Underhill, Esq. and others, and are particularly noticeable as good building sites.

LOT 4.

A Freehold Close of Arable Land, called "Blakely Field," and the road leading thereto from and out of the high road leading from the Sytch to Houndall, containing 2a. 0r. 18p. or thereabouts, and bounded by property belonging Mr. Hickford and lands belonging to the Rev. W. Dalton, the Rev. W. J. Heale, and Mr. Hill.

The above four lots are in the occupation of Mr. Hill.

LOT 5.

All that Field of Arable Land, known as the "Allotment," situate fronting the road leading from Wombourn into the Dudley and Bridgnorth turnpike road, having likewise a frontage to the Stafford and Worcester Canal, and containing 2a. or thereabouts.

1a. 0r. 13p. of this land is Freehold, and 27p. thereof is Leasehold for a term of one thousand years, commencing the 1st of May, 1665, at a pepper corn rent.

LOT 6.

The Navigation Inn and two Messuages, with the Stabling, Warehouses, and other Outbuildings, and the very excellent and productive Garden Land thereto belonging, now in the occupation of Mr. Richard Deans and his under-tenants.

This lot is situate at Houndall, on the side of the Stafford and Worcester Canal, to which it has a large frontage, and is bounded by the road leading from Houndall to Wombourn, and by lands of the Rev. Mr. Cornelius Cartwright, ...

1 rood and 25p. of this lot is Freehold, and the residue, namely, 15 yards in breadth and 37 yards in length (being the portion now occupied as the Navigation Inn and Buildings adjoining,) is Leasehold for one thousand years, commencing the 1st May, 1665, at a pepper corn rent.

LOT 7.

A Freehold Piece of Arable Land, called "Hatch Heath," fronting the road leading from Houndall to Wombourn and the New Inn, containing 2 roods and 16p. or thereabouts, bounded by lands of the Rev. W. Dalton, and occupied by Mr. Deans.

LOT 8.

A Freehold Piece of Land, known as "Harriett's Hedge," now occupied in Garden Allotments, having a frontage to the road leading from Houndall to Wombourn and the New Inn, and having also a frontage to the road leading from Gigity Bridge to Wombourn, containing 1a. 1r. 28p. or thereabouts, and bounded by lands of the Rev. W. Dalton and the Rev. W. J. Heale, and now in the several occupations of John Matthews, Edward Law, Charles Johnson, Richard Deans, and others.

LOT 9.

All that Freehold Messuage, with the Appurtenances and the Garden thereto belonging, situate in Over Street, in Wombourn, fronting the road leading towards the Church, and now in the occupation of Samuel Deans, and containing 21p. or thereabouts. This lot adjoins property of Mr. E. Powney and a foot road leading towards the Houndall and Wolverhampton Road.

LOT 10.

Four Freehold Dwelling Houses, with the Barn, Outbuildings, Garden Land, and Appurtenances thereto, now in the several occupations of Henry Bassano, Edward Law, Thomas Deans, and Hannah Evans, situate in Wombourn, at the corner of the road leading towards the Church and also to the road leading to Gigity Bridge, and adjoining properties belonging to the Rev. W. Dalton and Mr. James Aston, containing, including the site of the buildings, 36p. or thereabouts.

LOT 11.

Three Freehold Cottages, with the Nail Shops, Appurtenances, and Gardens thereto, situate at the opposite corner of the road leading to Gigity Bridge and near to the road leading towards the Church, and now in the occupations of John Horton, Charles Johnson, and John Matthews, and adjoining properties of Mr. James Aston and Mr. E. Hayes, containing, including the site of the buildings, 25½p. or thereabouts.

LOT 12.

Three Freehold Cottages, Nail Shop and Gardens thereto, situate near to Lot 11, and now in the occupations of James Cartwright and John Deans, and the other void. This lot contains, including the site of the buildings thereon, 22p. or thereabouts.

Further particulars and lithographic plans may be had of Mr. JOHN RILEY, Solicitor, Queen Street; Messrs. TIMMIS and WOODCOCK, Surveyors; or the AUCTIONEERS, Darlington Street, all of Wolverhampton.

An outing to Highgate Common for Wombourne children, organized by Wombourne Labour Party during the late 1940s.

Acknowledgements

We wish to record our gratitude to the many kind people who lent photographs and documents, for inclusion in this book. We were amazed to discover the number of wonderful pictorial records that exist.

The following people loaned \graphs or generously gave help in various ways.

Ted and Dorothy Bailey, Joan Beedle, Harry and Sylvia Blewitt, Jim Boulton, Ian Bratt, David Burton-Pye (South Staffs County Council), Olive Cartwright, Christine Clifford, Chris Davis, John and Eileen Disley, Elsie Edwards, Alan Edwards, Trixie Firth, Gwen Fisher, Jack and Jean Gash, May Griffiths, Colin Hardwick, Sue Harkness (Blakeley Heath Primary School: Head Teacher Pat Godby), Mary Jennings, Barbara Lander, Don Linney, Guy and Ann Morse-Brown, Kath Ogden, Reg Parnwell, John and Doreen Pike, Ted Powell, D.J. Powell, Fred and Jean Rogers, Dorien Russell, Helen Standish-Bevan, Gill Stuffins, Peter Tarnawskyi (Westfield Primary School: Head Teacher John Smith), Harvey Trott, Tony Unwin, Tony and Betty Vernon and Karen, Geoff Ward, John and Chris Whatton, Keith Wilson.

Last but by no means least, we should like to thank members of our families for their support and assistance.